Creative Chickens

Coloring Book for Chicken Lovers

Illustrated by Kerrie Hubbard

Every once in awhile a chicken enters
your life and changes
EVERYTHING.

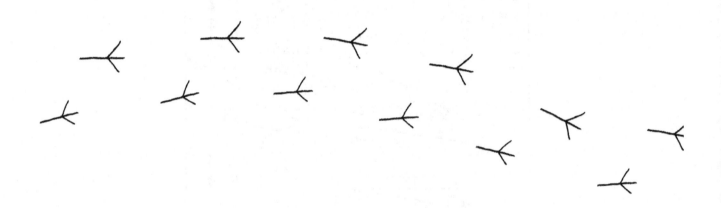

For more information including free downloads, please visit:
www.kerriehubbard.com
www.citygirlfarming.com

ISBN-13: 978-1537193656
ISBN-10: 1537193651

Dedication:

To my friend, Teresa, who began collecting my hand drawn books
before I knew how to draw.

Colored By:

_____

Date Started:

_____

Date Finished:

_____

Stan and Millie flew their city coop for life in the country.

Jess knew she was the cat's pajamas

(but she tried not to let it go to her head).

Regard it as just as desirable

to build a chicken house

as to build a cathedral.

-Frank Lloyd Wright

Happiness is a chicken to hug.

Lucy was feeling all "worm" and fuzzy.

The Mother Hen of Mother Hens.

Waiting for Thursday.

Every chick needs salt in her toes and sand in her feathers.

Lois regretted the 4 boxes

of chocolate covered worms

she ate before the party.

Marge dreamed for the day she'd set off

on the high seas of adventure.

Fresh as a chicken wearing daisies.

The best kind of love is the unexpected kind.

Harriet waited all her life for this moment to LEAP

(but suddenly it seemed very high).

Acorn was a little nutty, but in a loveable sort of way.

Thankfully there is no cure for O.C.D.

(Obsessive Chicken Disorder)

Florence was a bit complicated.

The path to his heart was paved with chicken prints.

"That's it" she said,

"I'm going to become

a chicken lady."

Thelma and Barley agreed

no fence was high enough to

keep them from love.

Happiness is a good night's sleep

on the roost with the one you love.

The following pages contain the original 20 full-page images in 4x6 size

(suitable for framing, gift giving, card making or anything your heart desires)

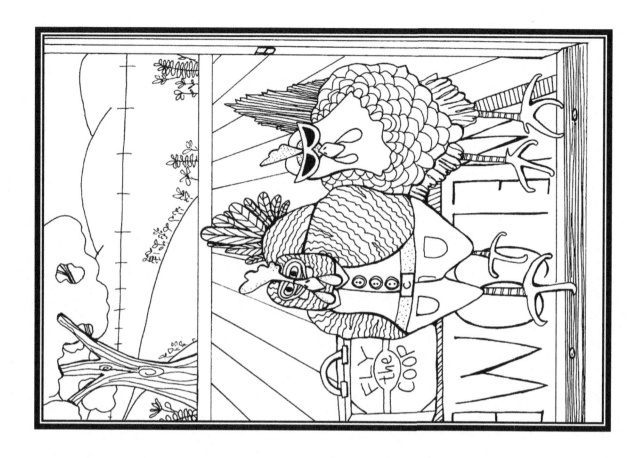

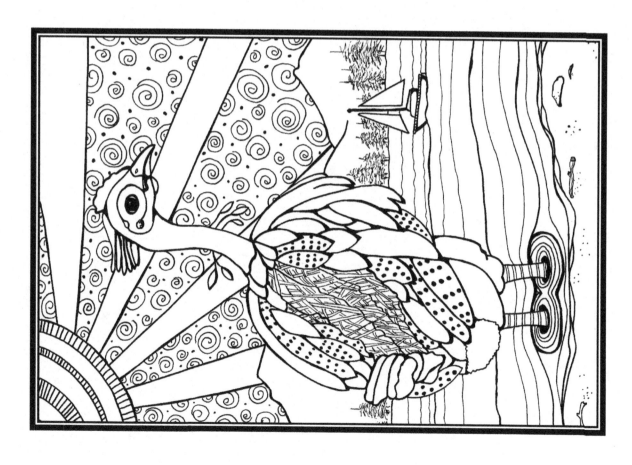

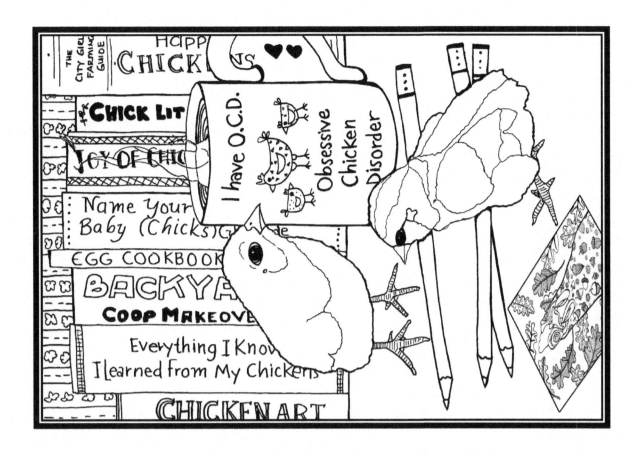

Thank you for supporting my crazy chicken loving dreams. If you enjoyed this coloring book,
please consider rating it on Amazon. I'd really appreciate it.

Come say hi on Facebook at CityGirlFarming and KerrieHubbardArt.

-Kerrie

Made in the USA
Middletown, DE
21 January 2020